William J. Cummins

The Turkish Bath

William J. Cummins

The Turkish Bath

ISBN/EAN: 9783337294175

Printed in Europe, USA, Canada, Australia, Japan

Cover: Foto ©Thomas Meinert / pixelio.de

More available books at **www.hansebooks.com**

THE

TURKISH BATH.

BY

WM. J. CUMMINS, M.D., EDINBURGH,

MEMBER OF THE ROYAL COLLEGE OF SURGEONS, EDINBURGH, ETC.,
PHYSICIAN TO THE CORK DISPENSARY,
LATE PHYSICIAN DEPOT MILITARY HOSPITALS, CORK,
FORMERLY SURGEON WEST INDIA ROYAL MAIL COMPANY.

Author of Essays

ON " DANGEROUS SYMPTOMS IN FEVER,"
ON " THE PATHOLOGY AND TREATMENT OF YELLOW FEVER,"
ON " PARAPLEGIA FROM ARTERITIS,"
" CONTAGION," ETC., ETC.

Re-printed from " The Dublin Hospital Gazette."

DUBLIN:
JOHN M. O'TOOLE, 13, HAWKINS'-STREET,
AND 6 & 7, GREAT BRUNSWICK-STREET.
1860.

PREFACE.

It is now nearly three months since I first read the following essay before the "Cork Medical and Surgical Association," where it afforded subject for most interesting discussion at three unusually large meetings. My best thanks are due to the President and Council of the Association for waiving the ordinary routine of business, which had hitherto limited the consideration of papers to a single meeting; at the same time it is only fair for me to notify that, as I preferred publishing the essay in a separate form to awaiting the issue of the Society's volume of Transactions (which cannot appear until mid-summer), the Association is in no way responsible for the matter I have brought forward. On myself personally rests all the odium, if odium there be, of advocating, on scientific principles, the judicious use of the Turkish Bath.

I believe I may safely leave myself in the hands of my Medical brethren, who will not fail to believe that my object in writing on this subject has been simply to advance the cause of truth, and to accelerate the transit into the hands of the profession of a most powerful agent, which, used without their guidance and direction, may be productive of evil. I am aware that before my paper appeared, some of the most eminent medical men in Cork had prescribed the Bath with benefit to their patients; but I am aware also that many, indeed, I may say the large majority, are opposed to it.

This paper does not profess to be a practical one ; it is simply a treatise on the general applicability of the Bath, and is not illustrated by a single case.

I know that it is, to a certain extent, imperfect without a well-selected list of cases in which the Bath has been used, and its effects carefully watched, being appended to it ; but I fear that until the Bath has been introduced into some of our hospitals, where it can be used in the treatment of the poorer classes, its practical value must remain buried in obscurity.

BLACKROCK, CORK,
April 5th, 1860.

THE TURKISH BATH.

It is little more than a century since the celebrated Lady Mary Wortley Montague, writing from Adrianople, in her own pleasant style, quotes the saying of the French ambassador : "They take the small-pox here by way of diversion, as they take the waters in other countries." A few years later she introduced the Turkish practice of inoculation for small-pox into England, and thereby struck the first deadly blow at the ravages of that loathsome disease, which, followed up and replaced by vaccination, has comparatively exterminated one of the greatest scourges that ever afflicted the human race.

Now again Turkey seems to have added a most powerful engine to the means already at the disposal of medical science—I allude to the Turkish bath — and although it has not as yet been endorsed by the Profession as a body, the time is fast approaching, I think, when every hospital, infirmary, and union will have its bath as a necessary addendum. Already private baths flourish and are well supported in many parts of the kingdom, and public as well as, to a certain extent, medical feeling seeks further information regarding their prophylactic and therapeutic value.

It is a trite observation that our Profession is generally slow to adopt any new sanitary agent, and fortunate it is for the public that, within certain limits, it should be so ; for it is not only becoming the dignity of so scientific a body to exercise the utmost discretion, but it is absolutely necessary, in its capacity as guardian of the public health, to restrain the many who, like the Athenians of old, spend their time in little else than seeing and hearing new things, from adopting the numerous cloaks for empiricism that have been continually bubbling and bursting in the newspapers of the nineteeth century.

It is our province to investigate such matters for the public, to bring sound physiological and pathological principles, with all the researches and discoveries that have enriched modern medicine, to bear upon them, and then to reject or adopt them according as they stand these tests, and a subsequent one of practical operation and clinical study. In such a spirit and with such intentions, I shall bring my best powers, feeble though they be, to bear upon my subject, merely premising, what it is hardly necessary to say, that I shall treat of the Turkish bath simply as an adjunct to medical treatment, never contemplating for a moment that it or any other agent is of universal application, or, in other words, that most absurd and unscientific of all things, that elixir vitæ of modern empirics—a panacea.

My first knowledge of this bath was derived from a paper read before the Royal Dublin Society, by Dr.

Haughton, on the 26th of March, 1858, and published in the DUBLIN HOSPITAL GAZETTE of the following month. I was greatly struck with it at the time, and hearing subsequently that baths had been erected in Cork and Passage, I took an early opportunity of testing its effects on my own person, the result being so satisfactory that I cautiously proceeded to give it a trial with such of my patients as I thought likely to derive benefit from it ; and I may add, that with increased experience of its effects my confidence in its value has gone on progressing.

I shall now proceed to give a brief description of the bath, taking as my model the very elegant one at Grenville-place : —

It consists of three large well-ventilated apartments, the outside one open to and at the temperature of the external atmosphere ; in the latter are placed couches of a peculiar construction, well calculated to relax the muscles and afford comfort and ease ; the second chamber is heated to about 100° or 110;° the light in it is partially obscured, and ordinary couches surround it on all sides, some of which are curtained off for invalids who may desire privacy. Communicating with this by a wide door is the third chamber, of somewhat smaller dimensions, and heated to about 140° or 150°; in its centre is placed a bench covered with wood, on which the bather may recline and undergo the process of shampooing, if he so desires ; off this apartment are washing rooms, where cocks of hot and cold water open into a large basin, and can be

mixed at any temperature ; beyond these again is the
cold douche, which can be directed on any part of
the body, and its force regulated by a flexible tube.

The bather having undressed, wrapped himself in a
sheet, and put on wooden clogs, is first introduced into
the middle chamber, and reclines there or walks about
conversing with his friends [not forgetting to drink
an occasional glass of cold water, which the Ganymede
or Hebe, as the case may be, presents to each in turn]
for a variable period, generally about an hour, but
regulated entirely by the condition of the skin, as,
until it is soft and perspiring freely, it is not safe to
enter the hot room ; as soon as this is the case he
proceeds towards the inner chamber, and remains
there until he has perspired copiously for twenty
minutes or half an hour, drinking water constantly to
replace the aqueous part of the perspiration. He then
enters the washing room, and having carefully cooled
his head with tepid water, washes his body with an
unlimited quantity of the same, and then directs the
cold douche over every part except the head. It is
impossible for any one who has not experienced it to
conceive the pleasure afforded by this part of the
process. This being done, the hot room is again
remained in for a short time, when, passing through
the second apartment, the bather arrives at the first I
have described, where, lying at ease on one of its
peculiarly constructed couches, fanned by the cool
atmosphere, he almost realizes the sensations of
Coleridge's ancient mariner, when, after the long and

parching drought which had proved fatal to all his companions, it rains upon him while he sleeps, and waking, he exclaims :

"Sure I had drunken in my dreams, and still my body
  drank."
*   *   *   *   *
"I moved and could not feel my limbs, I was so light,
  almost
I thought that I had died in sleep, and was a blessed
  ghost."

And here the bath terminates ; the bather resumes his clothes, and goes forth invigorated and refreshed.

But, it may be asked, why are such complicated processes and such artificial means necessary for the well-being of man ? and why is not the simple cold water, with which Providence has blessed mankind, sufficient for the purification of his system ? I answer, because man has acquired artificial habits, because civilization has enabled him in a great measure to escape from the decree, which became a law of his economy after the fall, that " in the sweat of his brow man should eat bread," because exercise of mind has, to a great extent, superseded that of matter; because many poor creatures can never

"Feel as they used to feel
  Before they knew the woes of want,
  Or the walk that *costs a meal;*"

and further, because, combined with absence of the physical exercise, which is the natural stimulant of all the organs absorbent and exhalent, civilization has tended to associate mankind in large communities, and to multiply cities, with all the contaminating influences thereby engendered; slowly but surely does intramural vitiation of the atmosphere work its undermining influences upon the human frame; emanations from thousands of bodies fermenting and putrifying, producing and reproducing poisons of the most deadly kind, sometimes quickly received into the blood, causing typhus or some other rapidly fatal zymotic disease; at other times more slowly but not less surely contaminating the blood and disorganizing the tissues it supplies. Even the very breath we breathe over and over again, in crowded dwelling-houses, ill-ventilated sleeping apartments, and over-crowded public rooms, becomes poisonous, while the various kind of chemical manufactures lend their aid to taint the air, and render what ought to be the breath of life too often the source of disease and death; each and every one of these, and still more, the combinations of them that are found in the alleys and by-lanes of our cities, cry aloud for some powerful counteracting agency.

Again, we have intemperance in eating and drinking as a fruitful source of blood poisoning. We all know that the elementary composition of human food is of two kinds, azotized and non-azotized, the former rich in nitrogen, the latter in carbon, and that while the first is necessary for the formation and reproduction of tissue, the second is slowly consumed by oxygen for the maintenance of animal heat, or stored up in the cellular tissue in the shape of fat, to provide against sudden vicissitudes of temperature. But the refinements of modern cookery have very much superseded the natural cravings of the *system*, for it is to the cravings of a morbidly stimulated *stomach* that the rich man attends, overloading it with a quantity and quality of food which the *system* does not require, while its digestion is stimulated by libations rich in carbon. His poorer brother, on the contrary, ill-nourished by the food he can hardly provide, resorts to the public-house, with its liquid and fiery hydro-carbons, which stimulate the system to increased energy, and consequently increased waste, without supplying any reproducing material. In both cases, a poison is introduced into the system, for the quantity of nitrogen not required, and which cannot be converted into muscle or nerve, becomes a source of injury, or, in other words, a poison; while for the same reason the excess of carbon not required for the support of animal heat or stored up as fat bcomes poisonous.

Syphilis is another general source of blood poisoning. We hardly know the extent to which, directly or indirectly, it injuriously affects the human race, as it is only its most striking manifestations that come under our notice; but one thing we do know, that it is a most subtle and intractable poison, and may outlive its recognizable indications, and be communicated to the offspring many years after every taint was supposed to have been removed.

But it is unnecessary for me to go on multiplying the various sources of blood poisoning, which civilization, with its necessary consequences and its vices, has engendered—it is better at once to proceed to the effects of those blood poisons on the tissues and organs through which they are circulated.

Were it not that the lungs, skin, liver, and kidneys stand at the threshold of the system, like safety valves, removing the effete matters, which, in the ordinary course of decay and renovation of tissue, are continually received into the blood, life would soon terminate; and were it not that when blood poisons contaminate the system, those organs are capable of increased function, civilized humanity would soon be exterminated. It is truly wonderful how long any or every one of them may be overtaxed by the excretion of poisonous influences without becoming diseased; but sooner or later undue excitement of any organ must result in its exhaustion, followed by non-excretion and disorganization. This is, I believe, the pathology of many of those worn-out and debilitated victims of intemperance that haunt our city infirmaries and dispensaries, seeking and obtaining relief from medicines that stimulate the excreting organs to increased effort, followed by palliation, return to the old habits, renewed demand for medicines, and so on until organic disease commences, runs a rapid course, and closes the scene.

Now, when all the excreting organs are in full play, and when active exercise is used to keep them in vigour, the system is preserved tolerably free from the injurious effects of blood poisoning. We are amazed at the quantity of whiskey a Highlander can drink when among his native mountains ; and it is an enigma to us how our worthy ancestors used to drink habitually after dinner as much as would make us elevated for a week, without much evil resulting ; the reason is that they were keen sportsmen and active men, who spent the good old days on foot or on horseback in the open air, and the poison was eliminated almost as fast as it was imbibed. The air-cells of their lungs, with their vast excreting surface, which is estimated at thirty times greater than the whole surface of the body, were constantly distended with the pure atmosphere, and the alcoholic hydro-carbons rapidly united with the oxygen which had thus been received into the blood, and were eliminated as carbonic acid and aqueous vapour, while their skin, in full vigour, set free the same poisonous principles.* But in our day, when, combined with constant ingestion and

---

* Although I had read with great interest a valuable essay of Dr. Haughton's, I was not aware until to-day (March 30th) of the resemblance between this passage and one of his. In writing on a subject of this kind, it is impossible to acknowledge the source of all the physiology brought forward, as books long read and forgotten involuntarily influence the mind.

The facts I have advanced have been the subject of my thoughts some years, long before I read Dr. Haughton's paper, or thought of writing on the Turkish Bath; still, the credit of having first applied some of them to the question before us is undoubtedly his due, and had I been aware of it before, I should certainly have acknowledged it in my first publication.

absorption of contaminating influences, we lack the physical exercise which it was intended by our all-wise Creator should be the portion of man, and which, while it is his punishment, is at the same time his protection, the catalogue of disease has largely increased.

Modern investigation, aided by the microscope and analytic chemistry, has of late years demonstrated fatty degeneration of tissue to be one of our most frequent diseases, and we can trace the cause of this in taking into the system more hydrogen and carbon than can be set free by the excreting organs. These elements become deposited in the organs and tissues as fat, which replaces their parenchyma and paralyzes their functions, whence result fatty and waxy degeneration of the kidneys, the prolific source of dropsy, local inflammation, and apoplexy; fatty degeneration of the heart and liver, of the muscular tissue, of the ovum, and even of the very bones, as in that rare and curious disease, mollities ossium.

I do not say that this is the *only* source of fatty degeneration, as I believe that in peculiar states of the system the muscular fibre itself may undergo a metamorphosis into fat; but that it is an important cause, and a most rational explanation of a large proportion of the cases met with, will, I am sure, be admitted. Indeed, we have direct proof that such is the case in the result of the treatment to which geese are subjected, to prepare their livers for the celebrated "Strasbourg pâtés." The combination of forced muscular inaction, diminished respiration, high temperature, and hydro-carbonaceous food, causes that rapid deposit of fat in the cells of the liver so grateful to the epicurean taste. But besides those chronic diseases caused by the retention of carbon and hydrogen in the system, we have dysenteries and bilious diarrhœas caused by the same; they are met with most frequently after a hot summer, during which the external temperature being high, the same amount of carbonaceous combustion is not required for the maintenance of animal heat, while, by stimulating digestion, as much carbon is taken in as during the cold weather of winter, when much more is required. Again, an excess of nitrogen taken into the system may produce another class of diseases, such as hypertrophies, calculous affections, gout, skin eruptions, cancerous disorders, hypochondriasis, dropsies, and many others, some of the local developments of which are only attempts of nature to eliminate the poisons—for instance, gout and skin eruptions. We know how fearful are the consequences if we suddenly put a stop to these; how the poison is often carried back into the circulation, and deposited, perhaps, in some vital organ.

I have now detailed a few of the most prominent effects of some of the various poisons which the civilized man is continually taking into his system. In the country, of course, as their causes are in much less constant and active operation, we do not meet with them to the same extent, and, as a natural consequence, life is more prolonged. The following

statistics, given by Dr. Watson on Dr. Farr's calcula-
tion from returns made to the Registrar-General,
indicate this difference.   " In cities, as contrasted
with rural districts, the deaths from consumption are
increased 24 per cent. ; those from typhus, 55 ; those
from child-birth 59 per cent., and so of several other
disorders.   The diseases chiefly incidental to childhood
are twice as fatal in the city districts as they are in
the country.   The mean duration of life in the two
classes of districts differs nearly seventeen years, being
in the proportion of 59 years (country) to 38 years
(town)."

But before I leave this part of my subject, there is
one point more not unworthy of attention ; I mean the
facility with which changes effected in the constitu-
tion of man by external agencies become permanent
taints, capable of being handed down to his posterity.
This is an established fact, and could be largely
illustrated if necessary ; and surely it ought to afford
an additional reason for keeping our systems in the
purest possible condition by every means at our disposal.   Now, the scientific physician, who sees in the
structural changes revealed by post-mortem exami-
nations and demonstrated by the microscope, only
local manifestations of general disorder of the system,
induced by blood poisoning, can alone be in a position
to appreciate such a powerful prophylactic, such a
valuable substitute for the active exercise which
quickens all the bodily functions, as the Turkish
Bath.   I do not mean, however, to recommend the

bath as at all equal to active exercise ; a day's hunting,
shooting, or coursing in the country, will do the man
of sedentary habits more good than many baths, because
these sports call the lungs, as well as the skin, into
active play, and cause the inhalation of large quantities
of oxygen, which is the true chemical antidote to the
hydro-carbons; for it is in the virtue of those elements
when in excess, combining with the oxygen necessary
for the muscular and nervous tissues, that they act as
poisons ; as in a perfectly healthy condition of the
system, when nutrition and excretion are nicely
balanced, there is a definite relation between the
amount of hydro-carbons and oxygen in the system.
But every medical man of experience knows how
difficult, nay, impossible it is to combat the business
habits, or, still worse, the indolent habits, of the
majority of city men.   They may, indeed, be induced
to take what is called a " constitutional walk," but it
is a fallacy to suppose that any exercise short of that
which quickens the circulation and respiration, and
opens the pores for free perspiration, can be a sufficient
antidote to the poisonous influences generated in cities,
or by habits of intemperance ; although even the
moderate exercise of a walk is sufficient to increase the
quantity of carbon excreted by the lungs, as proved
by the following observations of Dr. Carpenter, which
also show the effect of injestion upon that excretion.
" A person who was excreting 145 grains of carbon
per hour while fasting and at rest, excreted 165 after-

dinner, and 190 after breakfast *and a walk*, while he excreted only 100 during sleep."

According to the calculations of Rocheux, there are about six hundred millions of air cells in the human lungs, and each one of these is distended with air about eighteen or twenty times in the minute ; there it is brought into mediate contact with the blood, which absorbs from it a large quantity of oxygen, permitting the carbonic acid which had been already formed at the expense of oxygen in the blood, as well as aqueous vapour, to escape. It is difficult to calculate the average quantity of carbon which is thus eliminated in the twenty-four hours, but it may be roughly estimated at about ten or eleven ounces when at rest, and one or two ounces more during moderate exercise. The oxygen received into the blood at the lungs is partially appropriated to the oxydation of matters set free by decay of the solid tissues, while the remainder combines with hydro-carbonaceous matters existing in the blood.

The skin is the next important eliminator of hydro-carbons from the blood. Its extensive surface is thickly studded over with sudoriferous and sebaceous glands, and is largely supplied with lymphatics. It has been estimated that there are no less than seven millions of pores opening upon it, and that the ducts of its glands, if placed in a straight line, would extend over twenty-eight miles. Through this extensive system of drainage there ought daily to distil, on

an average, more than twenty-one ounces of fluid,
holding, in solution, according to Anselmino, from a
half to one and a half per cent. of solid matters, con-
sisting of a protein compound in a state of incipient
decomposition, saline matters, and, under the influence
of high temperature, urea. Besides this eliminating
function of the skin, it is possessed of a power similar
to that of the lungs of absorbing oxygen and setting
free carbonic acid gas ; so that if the body is coated
with an impermeable varnish, death is speedily the
result from reduction of animal temperature and
non-aeration of the blood. It is this part of its
function which is so useful to the economy in reliev-
ing the lungs when overtaxed ; it explains what those
who train for gymnastic feats call " the second wind."

But the skin has another and equally important
function to perform in maintaining a moderate temperature, no matter how great the external heat to which
the living body is exposed. It is evaporation from
the cutaneous surface which keeps the living body
cool, and permits scarcely any appreciable increase of
its temperature when exposed to a heat sufficient to
cook an animal that has been killed, and thus lost the
ability to perspire.

The experiments demonstrating this fact, related
by Doctors Watson and Carpenter, are truly wonderful. One girl remained in an oven for ten minutes,
with the thermometer at 280° ; another for five
minutes, while it rose to 325°, or 113° above the boiling point of water. Others remained in while eggs were

roasted quite hard in twenty minutes, and beefsteaks were dressed in thirty-three minutes, and when air was blown upon the meat by means of bellows it was sufficiently cooked in thirteen minutes.

In all these experiments it was found that the animal heat, as ascertained by thermometers placed under the tongue, was scarcely increased at all, and none of the experimenters were in the smallest way injured.

We are told also by Carpenter that Chabert, called "the Fire King," was in the habit of entering an oven the temperature of which was from 400° to 600°.

It seems, however, that the lower animals cannot be exposed to anything like such high temperatures with impunity ; for a rabbit placed by Sir B. Brodie in an oven at not more than 150° died in a few minutes; and the experiments made by Fahrenheit, related by Boerhaave, tend to the same conclusion ; for of various animals shut up in a sugar-baker's stove at 140°, a sparrow died in less than seven minutes, a cat in rather more than a quarter of an hour, and a dog in about twenty-eight minutes. The only explanation, I think, of this difference between man and the lower animals in toleration of external heat is, that the feathers and hair of the latter prevent the rapid evaporation, and consequent evolution of caloric, which maintain the normal temperature of the " featherless biped," man ; for I have noticed when taking the Turkish Bath that the only part which feels unnaturally warm is the hair.

For the preservation of life under these high temperatures, it is necessary that the air should be perfectly dry, as if at a temperature of 325°, or even much lower, the air was saturated with moisture, instant death would be the result, as no evaporation could take place. It is in this particular that the Turkish Bath, as used in this country, is superior to that used in Turkey, where the air in the hottest room is rendered somewhat vapourous.*

* Since I read this paper at the Medical Society, I have seen Dr. Corrigan's letter to the Editor of the *Hospital Gazette*, enclosing a paper by Dr. Madden, on the Turkish Bath. Dr. Corrigan speaks of the improvement I have alluded to above, calling it "a serious and dangerous mistake," and says that when rectified, "these Baths (the Turkish), will become most useful medical adjuvants." Now, while I think the utmost deference is due to any expression of opinion by such an accomplished physician, I cannot agree with him that the Hammààm, as described by Dr. Madden, is either less dangerous, or likely to be more useful in disease than the one I have described, for heated *vapourous* air must of necessity *raise the temperature of the body and quicken the circulation, and must inevitably produce instant death at the boiling point of water, provided the saturation with vapour is complete*; while, as we have seen, no ill effect is produced by *dry* air at double the temperature of boiling water.

Dr. Corrigan's objections to taking hot dry air into the lungs would be unanswerable, were it possible to inhale air in that condition; but we all know very well that the exhalation from the mouth, fauces, and large bronchial tubes, renders the air *moist*, at the same time that it *robs it of caloric*, long before it reaches the air cells; in point of fact the only air that can be taken hot into the lungs is air *saturated with moisture*, and which cannot be rendered cool by evaporation.

In confirmation of this we have the experiments recorded by Dr. Watson, briefly alluded to above, as special mention is made of the fact that the experimenters *cooled their hands by blowing on*

Before I leave the consideration of the functions of the skin I shall give an extract from the most popular author of the day on human physiology. Dr. Carpenter says :—

" With regard to the functions of the skin taken altogether as a channel for the elimination of morbific matters from the blood, it is probable that they have been much under-rated, and that much more use might be made of it in the treatment of diseases—especially of such as depend upon the presence of some morbific matter in the circulating current—than is commonly thought advisable ; we see that nature frequently uses it for this purpose, a copious perspiration being often the turning-point or crisis of febrile diseases, removing the cause of the malady from the blood, and allowing the restorative powers free play.

" Again, certain forms of rheumatism are characterized by copious acid perspirations; and instead

them. Dr. Corrigan illustrates the position he has taken up by referring to an attempt at heating a college room by the Hypocaust. The result he has given was the one to be expected, for the room being filled with dry air which had become comparitively cold, failed to encourage exhalation, at the time that it robbed the mucous membranes of their moisture, and thus produced the disagreeable drying effects alluded to ; had it been the intention to have raised the temperature of the lecture-room to a degree *greater than that of the animal body*, as is done in the Turkish Bath, then the cases would have been parallel, but the result would have been far different. The same remarks apply to stoves, which are also alluded to.

The air of the Turkish Bath is not, however, absolutely dry, for a small but inappreciable amount of moisture is drawn from the recesses in which water is liberally used.

of endeavouring to check these we should rather encourage them, as the best means of freeing the blood from its undue accumulation of lactic acid ; and it is recorded that in the sweating sickness which spread throughout Europe in the sixteenth century no remedies seemed of any avail but diaphoretics, which, aiding the powers of nature, concurred with them to purify the blood of its morbific matter. The *hot air bath* in some cases, and the wet sheet, which, as used by hydropathists, is one of the most powerful of all diaphoretics, will be probably employed more extensively as therapeutic agents in proportion as the importance of acting on the skin, as an extensive collection of glandulæ, comes to be better understood. The absurdity of the hydropathic treatment consists in its indiscriminate application to a great variety of diseases."—*Manual of Physiology*, p. 474.

The kidneys seem to be principally of use in the economy, for the excretion of effete azotized matters resulting from the decomposition of nervous and muscular tissues, and consequently the quantity of urea which their secretion contains varies with the amount of bodily and mental exercise, as well as the quantity of azotized food taken ; the latter has also a marked effect upon the amount of uric acid in the urine, which is also morbidly increased when the due oxydation of the blood is interfered with. The same may be said of lactic and hippuric acids, which are occasionally found in considerable quantity as results of blood impurity.

The liver is an organ of great importance as an eliminator of hydro-carbons, although a large part of its secretion is re-absorbed into the blood ; and it may be mentioned that in living beings the amount of fat which the liver normally contains has an inverse relation to the activity of respiration. Thus, glancing at extremes, we find birds with livers almost destitute of fat, while in fishes it is a mass of oil.

The intestinal glandulæ are for the removal of putrescent matters from the system, but occasionally may become vicarious of other organs, and eliminate impurities of various kinds.

I have now glanced at the principal excretory organs of the body—those which are used by Nature (and may be used by the physician, who ought always be an imitator of Nature) for the purpose of separating from the blood the poisonous matters, which, whether introduced from without or generated within the body, are injurious to it.

If the action of the lungs ceases for a few moments death is the inevitable consequence ; if the skin is coated with an impermeable varnish, so as to suspend its functions for a few hours, the same result ensues ; while liver, lungs, and intestinal glandulæ require days of suspension before the final event takes place. By a comparison of this kind we arrive at the relative importance of each in the economy as a blood purifier; and while the lungs stand prominently forward, the skin is the only other organ that at all approaches it in importance, for the simple reason that a part of its function consists in the absorption of oxygen, which, from its effects on the animal system, may truly be called " the breath of life." The liver and kidneys may mutually relieve each other when overtaxed or disordered ; the lungs and skin may assist them both, and be, to a certain extent, also relieved by them. But the internal organs, not being in contact with the atmosphere, can never be vicarious of that most important function of all, the aeration of the blood.

While, therefore, the physician derives great benefit from increasing the action of the liver, kidneys, and intestinal glandulæ, experience as well as physiology prove to him how much more subservient increased action of the lungs and skin may be made to his great object, the curing of disease.

These are admitted facts ; but we find it a difficult matter to induce our patients to take exercise, which is almost the only way of increasing the action of the lungs, or to avoid the impure atmosphere which in cities diminishes the benefit of free respiration. Such being the case, we must only do the next best thing we can for them, viz., stimulate, or rather give free play to, the only set of organs which can act vicariously with the lungs, and these are to be found in the skin. Well, we do this ! We order ablutions of various kinds, sponge baths, tepid baths, warm baths, vapour baths, &c., &c., and they all do good, and great good ; but none of them is at all equal to the Turkish Bath, which, besides its eliminating power, combines the luxury of the warm bath with the genial and refresh-

ing influence of the tepid, the bracing effect of the
cold douche, and, better than all, the absorption of
oxygen.   But on this latter point I shall speak more
at large, when I come to treat of it as applicable to
the prevention of pulmonary consumption among those
who have had the misfortune to inherit a tendency to
that disease.

It has been objected to the Turkish Bath that it is
debilitating; and if we confound the effect of the perspiration it causes with that of the colliquative sweating of hectic fever, we could not fail to believe it so,
for we all know how enfeebling is the latter ; but there
is no parallel between the two ; for the bath never
causes that antecedent febrile paroxysm which is the
cause of the perspiration, as well as of the exhaustion
which accompanies the decline of the hectic exacer-
bation.

I doubt whether even the Sudatorium (as the hottest
room of the bath is called) is debilitating, except when
used very often, and even then practical results seem
to argue the contrary, as the bath attendants, who
spend a great part of their lives in it, not only do not
grow thin, but absolutely gain flesh and strength,
notwithstanding its so-called exhausting influences.

But however it may be with the Sudatorium, the
other parts of the bath tend only to strengthen and
brace the system, and used in the way I shall hereafter
mention it becomes a powerful tonic.   Hitherto I
have treated of the Turkish Bath principally as a
prophylactic, as an antidote to the artificial and social

life we lead, and to the various contaminating influences we breathe, imbibe, and absorb.

If a man is intemperate in eating or drinking, the best advice we can give him is to give up the bad habits; the next best is to obviate their ill effects by constant and active exercise ; but if he objects to both these, the next best is habitually to take Turkish Baths. Call it a choice of evils if you will, and undoubtedly it is so, for any artificial and acquired habit, no matter how necessary to the comfort or even health of the indivividual, is an evil ; but there is as great a contrast between the evil of the bath and that of the lingering sickness and premature death which it tends to prevent, as there is between swallowing a nauseous dose and that of the disease it is taken to cure.

I shall now pass on to the consideration of the bath as a therapeutic or curative agent ; but having already exceeded the limits I had assigned to myself, I shall have to be more brief than I should wish.

It will be remembered that there are six different agents employed in the Turkish Baths, viz., 1st, air at the temperature of 100° ; 2nd, air at the temperature of about 140° ; 3rd, tepid water; 4th, the cold douche ; 5th, air at its ordinary temperature ; and 6th, shampooing. Each of these should be used in different ways, under medical guidance, according to the conditions of disease present in any given case.

Now, when first the bather enters the apartment heated to 100° the sensation is rather unpleasant, being a disagreeable feeling of heat and closeness ; this, however, is only momentary, and is caused by the sudden transition from the atmosphere without. The system soon accommodates itself to the greater heat ; the skin becomes soft, and gentle perspiration breaks out from every part of the body. This naturally occurs much sooner in those who habitually attend to the skin, and are in the daily habit of taking a bath, than in the " great unwashed," who permit layer upon layer of dead epidermis to accumulate upon its surface. It occurs also much more readily upon the skin of those who have recently taken the Turkish Bath. But there are some individuals so skin-bound that the temperature of 100° fails to produce any sensible impression on the secretion of perspiration, and for these it would not only be extremely dangerous to approach a higher temperature, but even continuing in the outer apartment must tend to raise the temperature of the body, to quicken the circulation, and thus favour determinations of blood to the brain, or other internal organ.

It is not always necessary for such persons to give up the bath ; indeed, on the contrary, they are the very ones who most require it ; and it will be found that proceeding to the washing-room, again and again, if necessary, and carefully cleansing all the pores with tepid water, will be followed, on returning to the heated chamber, by a rapid outbreak of perspiration. Drinking cold water will also conduce to the same desirable result.

But to return : the use of the external hot chamber is twofold ; first, as I have said, to prepare for the greater heat of the sudatorium ; and, secondly, to stimulate the functions for the cold douche, in cases where the bath is necessary—*as a tonic* during convalescence from acute diseases, and in other debilitating conditions of the system.

We all know the benefit of raising the temperature of the body before cold water is applied to it in any form, because heat is so rapidly abstracted from the body by this medium that all power of reaction is soon lost, unless some extra heat has been previously generated within, or applied from without.   The best swimmer, if he has been shivering on a rock for some hours after a shipwreck, will almost immediately sink if he trusts himself to the sea ; while the sailor who has been actively exerting himself to save his ship, when obliged at last to have recourse to the watery element, strikes out boldly and hopefully, for the animal heat which exercise had generated within him resists for some time the influence of the low temperature, and gives him time to swim to the shore.   We recommend our patients to take a smart walk (short of fatigue) before going into the water, and we say to those who take a cold sponge bath on winter mornings, " Take it hot out of bed, before the cold has time to reduce the reactive powers."   Now, patients who are convalescing from acute disease, or are debilitated from any other cause, have not vigour enough in their systems to react against the reduction of temperature

which cold bathing implies. They come out of a bath
shivering, yawning, dispirited, their fingers and toes
dead and benumbed, and it takes half a day before the
circulation is perfectly restored. Under such circumstances, the most sanguine physician could hardly
expect benefit to his patient; and so the powerfully
tonic, bracing, and invigorating effect of cold applied
to the animal body is lost to the very class of sufferers
who most require it. It will be seen at a glance that
the Turkish Bath may be so prescribed as to supply the
needful here; for by the application of the air at
100° of heat for a short time to the enfeebled body,
it is brought, without being in the least taxed, to a
temperature capable of withstanding the shock, which
in its remote effects is so powerfully tonic.

As soon as the bather has remained long enough in
the outside hot room to prepare his skin for the sudatorium he may enter it, and it is then that the full
benefit of the bath as *an eliminator* is perceived;
for under a heat of 140° or 150° streams of perspiration flow freely from every pore, while the various
organic and inorganic matters naturally thrown off by
the cutaneous glandulæ, as well as urea or other
noxious matters that may happen to be held in solution by the blood, are thrown off in large quantities.

But it may be argued that this process must disturb
the economy of the system; that to supply the great
drain of aqueous fluid from the blood the skin will
draw upon the secretions, which are poured out upon
serous and mucous surfaces, and which are necessary

for the due performance of their functions, and that these being exhausted, the specific gravity of the blood will be increased, and its circulation retarded, as we find from similar causes in cholera ; or that from a relative increase of fibrine in the blood those effects will take place which in certain conditions of the system occasionally cause sudden death, by mechanically arresting the heart's action.

But such objections overrate altogether the drain caused by the sudatorium, forgetting that it is used only for a very limited period, and that we have always at hand the means of supplying the waste, and preserving the specific gravity of the blood intact by draughts of cold water, which we know may be taken up directly by the veins of the stomach, received into the circulation, and thrown out from it again in the shape of perspiration, all within the space of a very few moments. Besides which, the action of the skin and kidneys, being, to a certain extent, vicarious, the water about to be poured into the ureters will be turned off into the new channel before other fluids of the body are drawn upon.* The possible danger of increasing the functions of the skin at the expense of other organs, should, however, be always borne in mind, and should contra-indicate the sudatorium, when any internal and necessary secretion, is

---

* If the drain of the sudatoriam was injurious to the system it would surely be indicated by thirst, as prolonged exercise and other conditions which expand the watery part of the blood, and such diseases as cholera, cause extreme thirst.

through disease, diminished; such, for instance, as that fruitful source of dyspepsia, diminished secretion of gastric juice, or the still more frequent torpor of the liver, resulting in habitual constipation, although the latter in some of its modifications may rather be benefited by the sudatorium, which, if used, would tend to remove congestion of the viscus, as well as to eliminate the matters which disease had rendered it unable to throw off. Such, however, are details which should be regulated by medical advice, in every individual case, and to which no general rules can invariably apply.

The sudatorium is contra-indicated during the performance of any of the great bodily functions which require the energies of the system to be directed towards any particular part of the economy. I mean digestion, pregnancy, lactation, and menstruation. The first of these requires repose of mind and body during its early stages, in order to concentrate all the energies upon a process so essential to the well-being of the system, and if exercise or study interfere with the due outpouring of gastric juice, surely the copious perspiration caused by the sudatorium would have a like effect.

We know that any drain from the body may become vicarious of menstruation, and interfere with the periodicity which is essential to the health of women, so that we may consider the Turkish Bath as inapplicable during the healthy performance of this function. But the possibility of the skin, unduly stimulated by the sudatorium, appropriating the function of other organs to itself, leads me on to its action as a derivative from other organs when congested or inflamed, and also as a substitute for other organs, when they happen to be rendered unfit for service by disease.

Now, while the Turkish Bath may be useful in inflammation of any of the internal organs, as a derivative, it is only perhaps in diseases of the liver and kidneys that it acts in both capacities ; for while it draws the blood towards the surface away from these, it also takes on their function of eliminating the matters which they, in the healthy condition, would have set free, and is thus of double benefit. We have seen that in perfect health the skin excretes carbon and hydrogen to a certain extent, and that under the influence of high temperature it may throw off urea. Surely, then, it is only for us to give that impulse to the skin excretion, which the Turkish Bath is capable of, to make it a powerful means of obviating the dangers of these diseases. I have already spoken of the bath as a means of *preventing* one cause of fatty degeneration of various organs, especially of the liver and kidneys ; and here now I go further and say that it is one of the most powerful auxiliaries we possess in the *treatment* of these diseases. 1st. because both tend to retain noxious matters in the blood which the sudatorium is capable of removing through the skin. What is the chief danger in the various forms of Bright's disease of the kidneys ? Is

it not nonelimination of urea—that condition of blood
called uræmia ?   But it may be said apoplexy is very
common in this disease, and the Turkish Bath should
not be used when there is a tendency to apoplexy.
True !   But what is the chief cause of the apoplexy
here ?   Is it not the uræmia?* and will not the skin,
under the influence of heat, eliminate urea, and thus,
in preventing further toxæmia, if not removing that
already present, prevent also the apoplexy which
depends upon it.

Second. Both diseases tend to cause dropsy.

Now, in hepatic dropsy hydrogogue cathartics are
undoubtedly the most powerful means of cure at our
disposal, as they *directly* empty the portal veins.
But in renal dropsy, in which we cannot generally
use diuretics, and in which there is often an irritable
condition of bowels, the most powerful of all remedies

---

* In cases of renal disease, unaccompanied with any considerable discharge of by the albumen kidneys, retention of urea is
perhaps the only cause of the toxæmia so constantly associated
with it.   Where the albumen is drained off in large quantities,
however, another cause exists.   "Dr. Owen Rees has suggested
that the remarkable diminution of blood discs in cases of albumen
urea may be due to their distention in consequence of the draining
away of albumen from the blood, and its subsequent reduction to
a very watery state.   The same circumstances may also prevent
their re-development from chyle and lymph, both in these cases
and chlorosis."—*Williams' Principles of Medicine*, p. 168 and 169.

If this theory is correct, we have another indication for the use
of the Turkish Bath in both renal disease and chlorosis, as the
repeated use of the sudatorium *without drinking water* would tend
to increase the specific gravity of the blood, and thus prevent the
blood corpuscles from becoming distended by endosmosis, and
their consequent bursting and obliteration.

are diaphoretics. But the misfortune is that most medicines of this class are also diuretics, and as such are generally contra-indicated in renal disease. The vapour bath and warm bath, both diaphoretic to a certain extent, are very debilitating when frequently used, besides being greatly inferior as diaphoretics to the Turkish Bath, so that we are driven to the use of the latter. Most high authorities on renal disease recommend the hot-air bath in its treatment as one of the most powerful means at our disposal, and a late author (Dr. Todd) says that we may prevent its debilitating effects by following it up with a cold douche. Now, what is this but the Turkish Bath?

Third. As a *derivative* in diseases of those organs. There is perhaps no more certain law in disease than that an organ overtaxed for any considerable period is sure to suffer. Now, the liver and kidneys are no exceptions to this, and they are both prone to congestions and inflammations from this cause.

Why, half, if not all, the dysenterics of tropical climates proceed from the congestion of an overtaxed liver ; and pathologists are, I believe, now agreed that acute dropsy, as well as that form met with after scarlatina, is caused by acute desquamative nephritis, and in both cases it is conditions of the skin that are the immediate cause of the invasion of the disease.

The soft and perspiring skin of the tropical resident is exposed to the damp chill of the night air ; he is attacked with hepatitis, and dysentery follows from retardation of the portal circulation. The drunkard in this country lies all night under the cold air, perhaps in a ditch, with his skin chilled to the last degree, and wakes up next morning with inflammation of the kidney and dropsy. The skin of the scarlatina patient is desquamating ; he catches cold, the surface is chilled, and he suffers from the same disease. The extra work of the internal organs, entailed by arrest of cutaneous elimination, is the common cause of disease in them all ; and the means which best afford relief to the diseased organs are those which most successfully act upon the skin. There can be little doubt that such is to be found in the Turkish Bath.

But I should be far from trusting to the bath *alone* in any of these diseases, or even to giving it the first place in *acute* diseases of internal organs, as in such the tendency to disorganization is so rapid that far more potent means are necessary, some of which are incompatible with the sudatorium, which must be omitted or postponed when they require to be prescribed.

AS AN ELIMINATOR OF THE BLOOD-POISONS WHICH CAUSE GOUT, RHEUMATISM, SECONDARY SYPHILIS, AND KINDRED DISEASES.*

I have already spoken of the bath as a means of *preventing* those diseases which depend upon peculiar conditions of the blood.

* Speaking of the use of the hot air bath, Dr. Haughton makes the following remarks; " The medical practitioner will find it an invaluable addition to other treatment in all cases of blood-poisoning, whether by uric acid, (as in gout and gravel), by

In most of these the toxæmia is gradually developed, and may not produce any manifest effect upon the general health, until, having approached a culminating point, or else upon the application of some exciting cause, a sudden paroxysm of the disease is a result of the poison seizing upon some joint, or it may be some other tissue or organ, and endeavouring to eliminate itself by producing inflammation.

Now, it is during the latent condition of these affections, or in the *very earliest* stage of the acute attack, that the Turkish Bath should be recommended, for when the disease is fully established the pain is so great as often to render it scarcely admissible. Both gout and rheumatism we know depend upon an excess of acid in the blood—the one on lithic acid, the other on lactic acid ; and the most rational and successful mode of treatment is generally believed to be the alkaline, which directly neutralizes the poison. But the new compounds formed require to be eliminated ; and we should aid the efforts of nature towards this end by medicines and other means, looking forward to the bath as the most powerful that can be used as soon as the patient is sufficiently recovered to be moved. The use of the bath during convalescence from acute rheumatism will generally have the effect of preventing the disease from degenerating into that chronic inveterate form which has always been the opprobium

lactic acid, (as in rheumatism), by the hydrocarbons, (as in bilious diarrhœa), as also in those forms of disease which arise from a deficiency of nature's purifier, oxygen gas."

of medicine, while, for the treatment of the chronic
stage itself, there is, perhaps, no other single remedy
at all equal to it.

IN THE EARLY STAGES OF FEBRILE DISEASES.

The class of zymotic diseases is now, as its name
implies, generally believed to depend upon the introduction of a poisonous matter into the blood, by contagion or atmospheric influence, which differs from
other poisons in possessing the power of reproducing
itself, as a ferment, at the expense of some normal
constituent of the circulating fluid, until at length, in
a period varying according to the nature of the
individual disease, it contaminates the entire system,
and is subsequently thrown off by the supervention
of a sudden or gradual crisis.

During the first stages of this process, before the
blood has been entirely contaminated, or even while
yet the morbific matter is limited to the blood, I think
it is not impossible that the eliminating influence of
the Turkish Bath may be equal to expelling the poison,
and cutting short the disease. I have not used it in
diseases of this class, but is well worthy of a trial.
If once, however, a zymotic disease becomes firmly
established in the system it must run its course ; and,
laying aside all hopes of cutting it short, we should
direct our attention towards treating any local com-
plication that may arise, obviating the tendencies to
death, ensuring sleep, perfect cleanliness, and free
ventilation, reserving the use of the bath for the period

of convalescence, when it will be found an invaluable tonic and eliminator.

IN SKIN DISEASES.

I have not as yet had much experience of the bath in this class, but I am sure that in many of them it might be used with advantage ; for while the causes of skin diseases are very various, a large proportion of them certainly depend upon retention of the cutaneous excretion from neglect of ablution ; some also are only efforts of nature to expel a constitutional taint, and thus point to diaphoretics as their most natural cure ; some originate in scrofula, which, as I shall point out presently, is greatly benefited by the bath ; while all require as an essential adjunct to any treatment, the most perfect cleanliness of the skin.

But the constitutional origin of a large proportion of the most inveterate skin eruptions, and the cachectic condition which often accompanies them, indicate that tonics and special stimulants, as well as a careful regulation of diet, must be items in their treatment.

IN SCROFULOUS DISEASES.

This class, we all know, is caused by the tuberculous cachexia, a tendency to deposit in the organs and tissues of a peculiar unhealthy lymph, which may be the result of any causes which tend to depress the vital power, especially cold and damp, as also of a deficiency of oleaginous matters in the food, or a malappropriation of that which is taken into the system.

The indications of treatment in these diseases are, first, to protect against cold and damp; second, to supply the relative deficiency of oil (by cod liver oil, &c.); and third, to brace and invigorate the frame in every possible way.

Now the Turkish Bath, used in the way I have described, as a tonic, will be found a valuable addition to the means of carrying out the third indication; but when we take pulmonary consumption as the great representative of scrofulous affections, as the culminating point of the tubercular diathesis, we find a much more important use for the Turkish Bath. We know that this disease is eminently an hereditary one, and that with the tendency to tubercular deposit the parent often hands down to his offspring the narrow and contracted chest which tends to localize the disease within the thorax.

The consequence of this is imperfect oxydation of the blood, with its results, imperfect generation of animal heat, and feeble circulation. Now, cold is an important cause of struma, as illustrated by the numbers of negroes, monkeys, and other tropical aborigines, which fall victims to it when transplanted to this country; so that if in any way we can increase the heat-producing functions of those who have an hereditary predisposition to phthisis we do much towards securing them against its invasion. Now, the chemical union of carbon and hydrogen with oxygen, resulting in carbonic acid and water, is the chief source of animal heat; and when we adminster olcaginous

matters, such as cod-liver oil, we are introducing two
of the necessary elements of heat. But the lungs are
contracted, and cannot absorb sufficient oxygen; how
then are we to obtain it? Some of the latest
remedies discovered for consumption, the hydrophos-
phates of soda lime, as well as one of the oldest (which
has now fallen too much into disuse), chlorate of
potash, are rich in oxygen, and probably owe their
beneficial action principally, if not entirely, to this
principle.* But there is another source to which
physiology directs our attention, and which, I believe,
may be used so as almost entirely to counteract the
injurious effect of contracted chest. I have before
hinted at the part which the skin plays in ærating
the blood, and thus supporting animal heat. This
is so great in certain classes even of vertebrate
animals, such as the batrachia, whose skin is *soft, thin,
and moist*, that the cutaneous respiration is capable
of sustaining life for a considerable period; but even
in the human being, as Professor Scarlig ascertained,
the proportion of carbonic acid given off from the skin
is from one-thirtieth to one-sixtieth of that exhaled by
the lungs during the same period of time. "Moreover,"
(says Carpenter) "it has been ascertained not un-
frequently, that the livid tint of skin which supervenes

---

* Dr. Williams suggests for certain diseases depending upon
deficiency of oxygen, injecting into the veins matters holding
oxygen in loose combination, such as chlorates, nitrates, &c.; he
also speaks of the use of warm baths holding these matters in
solution. It seems to me that there is oxygen enough in the air
around us, if we would only open the pores to let it in.

in asphyxia, owing to the nonarterialization of blood in the lungs, has given place after death to the fresh hue of health, owing to the reddening of the blood in the cutaneous capillaries, by the action of the atmosphere upon them, *and it does not seem improbable that, in cases of obstruction to the due action of the lungs, the exhalation of carbonic acid through the skin may undergo considerable increase. Moreover, there is evidence that the interchange of gases between the air and the blood, through the skin, has an important share in keeping up the temperature of the body."—Carpenter's Principles of Physiology, p. 536.*

Physiology thus teaches us that the skin is the medium through which the efforts of the physician should be directed in order to support the animal heat, to stimulate the languid circulation, and to prevent the cold extremities, so often associated with, and in a great measure dependent on, contraction of the chest, and hereditary predisposition to consumption ; while comparative anatomy indicates the the condition of the skin, which best conduces towards the interchange of gases, which causes cutaneous æration of the blood, for we have seen that the batrachia, whose skin is *soft, thin, and moist,* are thereby rendered almost independent of pulmonary respiration. Can we produce such a condition of skin as this in our patients ? I believe the Turkish Bath is capable of doing so in a great measure, for while the hot air renders the skin *soft and moist,* the process of shampooing loosens and peels off the superficial layers of epidermic cells, thereby *thinning* the cuticle, while all together produce that almost batrachian condition of skin which absorbs oxygen gas, and sets free carbonic acid, during the time spent in the outer or cold chamber of the bath, as well as for hours and even days subsequently. It is true that the immediate effect of elevated temperature is to reduce absorption of oxygen and limit exhalation of carbonic acid gas, and that for this reason the hour or two spent in the heated air of the bath has the effect of, *for the time being*, retaining in the system, to a certain extent, the gases that should be eliminated. This, however, is far more than compensated by the enormous excretion of solid and fluid effete matters, during the first stages of the bath, combined with the subsequent interchange of gases which the last process causes ; yet it should lead us to avoid prescribing hot air in any of its modifications where advanced pulmonary disease has already carbonized the blood, and tinged the countenance and lips of that livid hue which too surely indicates that even its temporary increase might be attended with rapidly fatal consequences.*

AS A SEDATIVE IN IRRITATION OF THE SYSTEM, AND OF CERTAIN ORGANS.

There are many conditions of the nervous system in which, without actual disease being present, there is a

---

* The same may be said of cardiac disease, which, by directly or indirectly obstructing the flow of blood through the right side of the heart, gorges the venous circulation, and prevents due pulmonary æration of the blood.

morbid irritability of all the bodily functions, or of certain parts.

The *Materia Medica* is rich in remedies for such affections, while the warm bath and shower bath are most useful adjuncts to their treatment. The Turkish bath, however, is superior to either of them, when used without the sudatorium, as with the stimulant influence of air at 100° it combines the use of warm, tepid, and cold water, which may be used together or separately, according to the physician's prescription.

The subject I have chosen for this essay is one which might be lengthened almost interminably, as it branches off at every turn into the most interesting researches of physiology and pathology. I have endeavoured to be as brief as possible, and have, I fear omitted many important details ; but I am sure that, ere long, when, like Harvey's discovery of the circulation, Jenner's of vaccination, and others of many other great truths, which met with great opposition —when, I say, the Turkish Bath shall have triumphed over prejudices, and become a recognised sanatory and therapeutic agent, attached to all charitable institutions for the prevention and cure of disease, then the professors and teachers of medicine will be able to enunciate the results of experience at the bedside, and to enter into the close practical details of its application to different diseases in the various modes in which it can be prescribed.

I have no doubt it will be a subject of remark that I have represented the Turkish Bath as very widely

applicable in the treatment of disease ! It may even be
said that my advocacy of it falls little short of what
would be accorded to a panacea. This would be an
unfair mode of arguing against an agent the use of
which, in every case where I have recommended it, I
have endeavoured to explain on scientific principles.
But as it may be used, I shall answer it by saying that
the bath is one of those agents which are found by
experience to have a wide range of application in the
treatment of disease ; and there are several such, and
no physician thinks of condemning them because they
are such. Let me just mention leeches. Surely there
is hardly a disease to which the body is liable that I
may not say, in some stage or other, has been benefited by them ; and still no one thinks of discarding
the useful little creatures as a panacea. The same
might be said of blisters, warm baths, and a host of
others. But, really, it is descending from the high
position I have taken up for the Turkish Bath to take
notice of such frivolous objections.

I have treated of the sudatorium as incompatible
with *certain classes* of medicines, as it eliminates them
by the skin as fast as they are absorbed, and before
their beneficial effect is produced. This does not apply,
however, to the use of the bath in any other way than
as an eliminator and derivative, because the sudatorium
is not necessary, and should not be used except when
these effects are desired.

I have put the words "*certain classes*" in italics in
order to show that I do not believe even the suda-

torium to be incompatible with medicine *generally;*
for, on the contrary, it will sometimes be found that
it creates a necessity for medicine by determining too
much to the surface away from internal organs.

The use of the bath as a tonic, or for facilitating the
absorption of oxygen, is, however, free from any objec-
tion of this kind.

I have spoken of habitual use of the bath as a choice
of evils for persons of sedentary habits, who either
cannot or will not take exercise.

It is used in this way rather to prevent than cure
disease, and no more requires the constant surveillance
of the physician than a cold bath or warm bath when
used during health.

But it is far otherwise when, disease being present
in the system, the bath is required as an agent towards
its cure ; for the endless varieties which disease
assumes, and the countless modifications of symptoms
which are daily met, require to be carefully noted by
a skilful medical man, and the bath suspended, repre-
scribed in another form, continued, or omitted altogether, according to the effect it has produced, or the
new phases of disease that may have arisen. The
bath may be very useful in certain stages of a disease,
and very injurious in others : it may do great good
combined with certain medicines, and great harm with
others, or with none at all. Diseases cannot be prescribed for by their names, because constitutional
peculiarity, as well as varieties in symptoms and
stages, must all be taken into account. carefully

weighed and reasoned on by a mind well educated in physiology and pathology, and stored with facts that experience alone can accumulate.

The Turkish Bath, used in any of its various forms for the treatment of disease, is a powerful agent, and if ill directed may be productive of the worst results ; and although I believe many of the stories continually circulated regarding ill effects said to have occurred from the use of the bath in this city, are entitled to as much credence as the famous tales of the vaccinated "bellowing like bulls," "growing horns from their foreheads," &c., that were diligently circulated on *the best authority*, and attributed to the introduction of cow diseases into the system of the human being in the days of Jenner, yet there can be little doubt that the indiscriminate application of the bath in various diseases that have been too common here must have been attended with mischievous results. I shall illustrate this matter in a very simple way.

A person in perfect health may take fifteen or twenty drops of laudanum without the least danger. The same man, during fever, and after nights of sleepless agony, when his life is vibrating in the balance, may be restored to his anxious friends by the same dose; while at a later period, perhaps, if suffering from want of sleep, from determination of blood to the head, he is induced to swallow the same dose, he too surely sinks into the sleep that knows no waking, his life the sacrifice of that very agent which had before proved his salvation. How needful, then, are the services of the enlightened physician to watch over any means that may be used in disease! The more useful they are the more powerful over disease they must be; and the more powerful the more necessary is the supervision of an educated eye. The Turkish Bath is powerful in disease, and for that very reason the Turkish Bath should be regularly prescribed, and its effects watched by the physician.

THE END.